Lead Guitar Licks
The Basics and Beyond by Joshua Ray

Cover photo courtesy of Robert M. Knight
Amplifiers used in video courtesy of Rick Fuhry

To access video visit:
www.halleonard.com/mylibrary

Enter Code
7075-4372-1150-8762

ISBN 978-1-4803-5407-4

HAL•LEONARD®
CORPORATION
7777 W. BLUEMOUND RD. P.O. BOX 13819 MILWAUKEE, WI 53213

In Australia Contact:
Hal Leonard Australia Pty. Ltd.
4 Lentara Court
Cheltenham, Victoria, 3192 Australia
Email: ausadmin@halleonard.com.au

Visit Hal Leonard Online at
www.halleonard.com

Contents

Introduction

Welcome to *Lead Guitar Licks—The Basics and Beyond!* In this video and book, I will be showing you many different concepts to improve your improvisational abilities. We will focus on phrasing, timing, technique, motif building, and conceptual thinking, among many other things. I'll talk about approaches to your instrument, as well as developing your own style. The goal of this video and book is to teach you to become your *own* guitar teacher, ensuring that you have the skills to continue improving and developing as long as you desire. Let's get started!

—Joshua Ray

About the Video

The accompanying videos can be accessed for download or streaming by visiting **www.halleonard.com/mylibrary** and entering the code found on page 1. Every example played in the videos includes a corresponding transcription in the book!

Lick 1

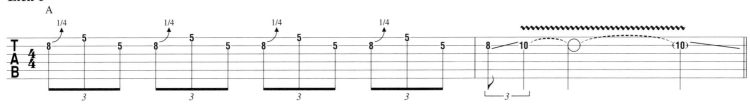

A Minor Pentatonic Scale (Pattern 1)

Lick 1, Variation 1

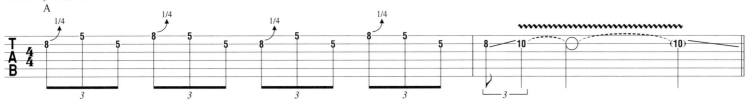

Lick 1, Variation 2

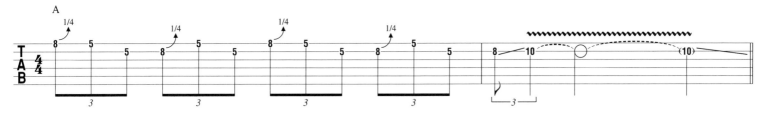

Lick 1, Variation 3

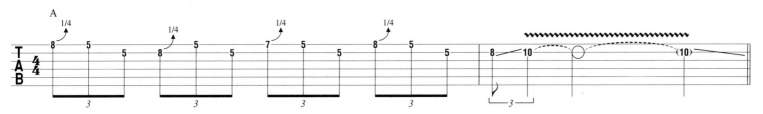

Lick 1, Variation 4

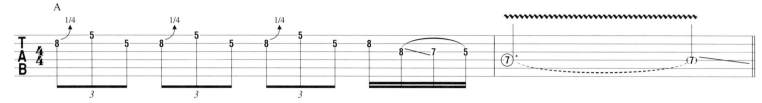

A Blues Scale

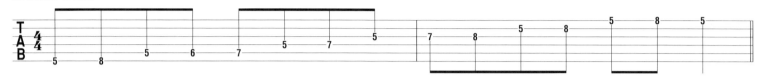

Lick 1: Creating Seamless Flow

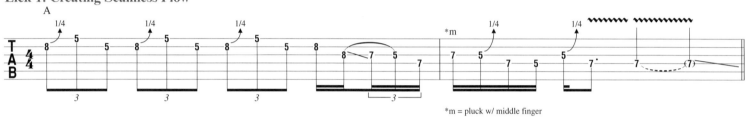

*m = pluck w/ middle finger

Lick 1, Variation 5

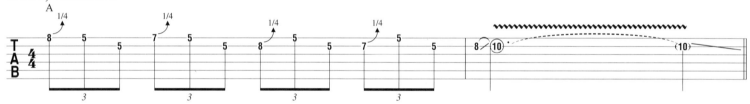

A Dorian Scale

Lick 2

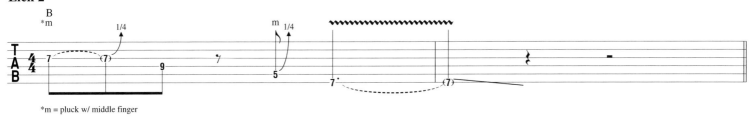

*m = pluck w/ middle finger

Lick 2, Variation 1

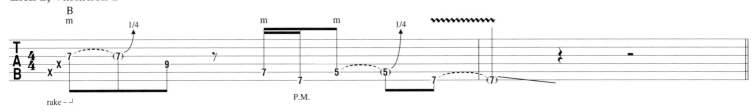

Lick 2, Variation 2

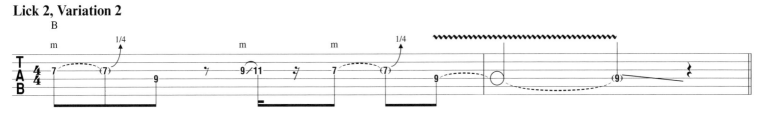

Lick 2, Variation 2: Creating Subtle Variations

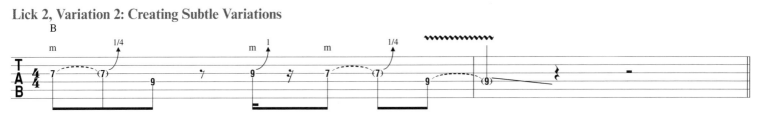

Lick 2, Variation 3

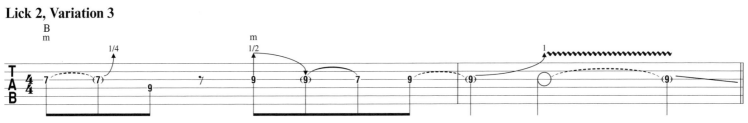

Lick 2, Variation 4

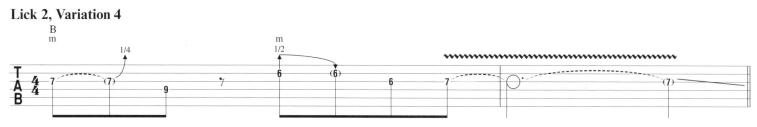

Lick 3

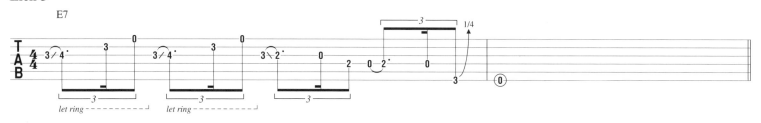

Lick 3, Variation 1

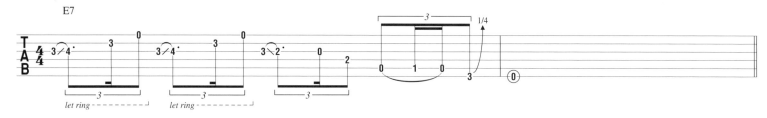

Lick 3, Variation 2

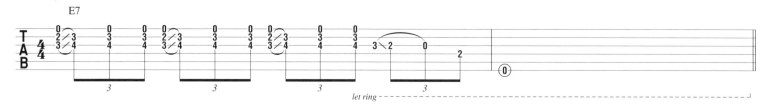

Lick 3, Variation 3

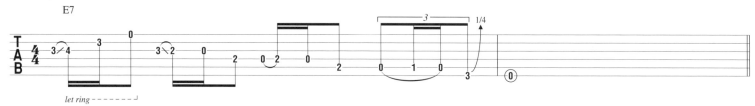

Lick 4

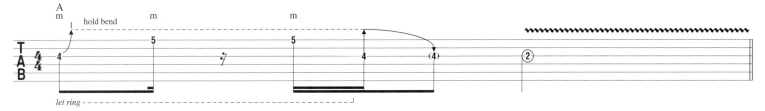

Lick 4, Variation 1

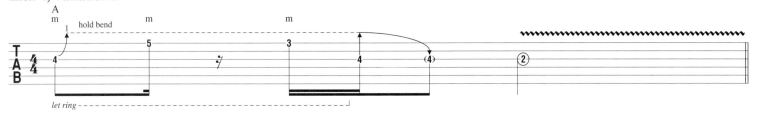

Lick 4, Variation 2

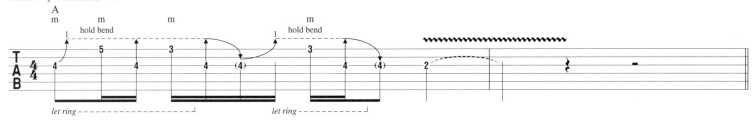

Lick 4, Variation 3

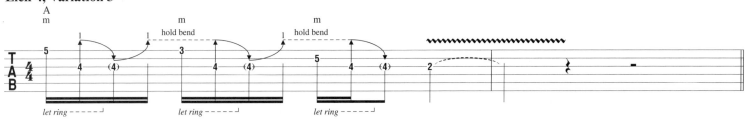

Lick 4, Variation 4

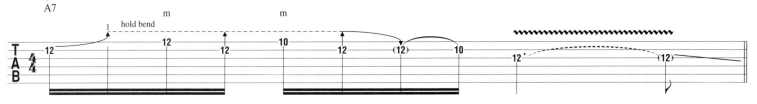

Lick 5

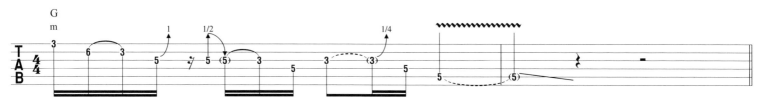

Lick 5, Variation 1

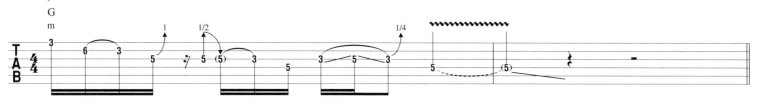

Lick 5, Variation 2

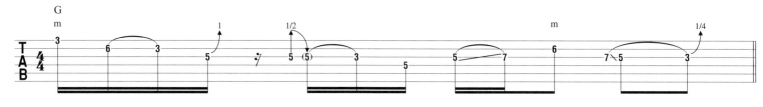

Lick 6

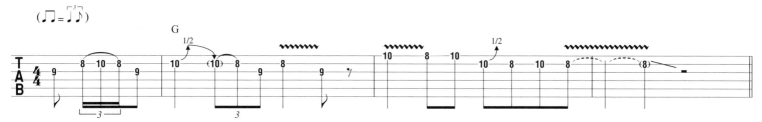

B.B. King Box (in G)

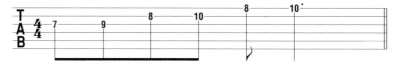

Lick 6, Variation 1

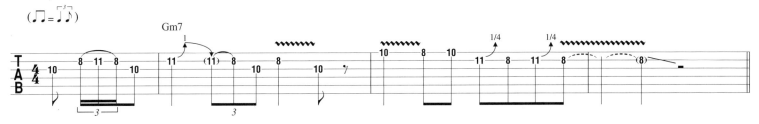

Lick 6, Variation 2

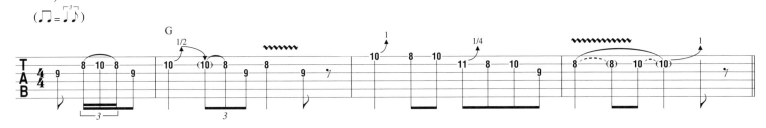

Lick 7

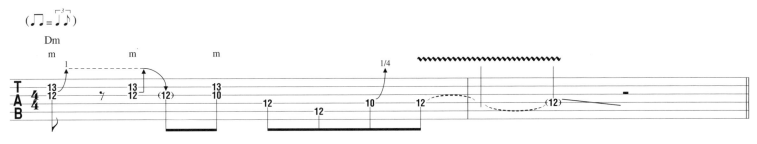

Lick 7, Variation 1

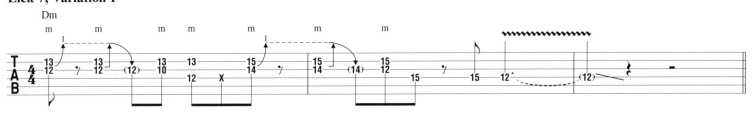

Lick 7, Variation 2

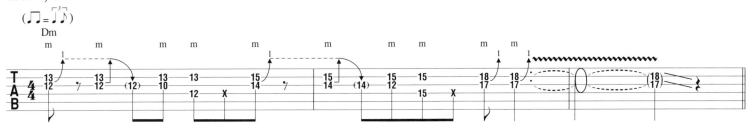

Lick 7, Variation 3

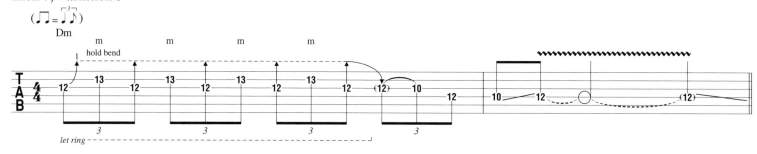

Lick 8

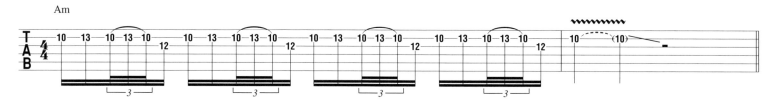

A Minor Pentatonic Scale (Pattern 3)

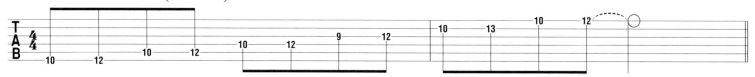

Lick 8, Variation 1

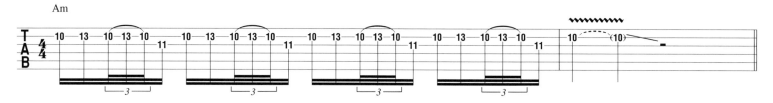

Lick 8, Variation 2

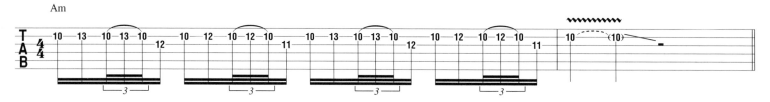

Lick 8, Variation 3

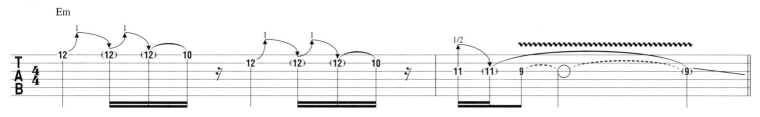

Lick 9

E Minor Pentatonic Scale (Pattern 5)

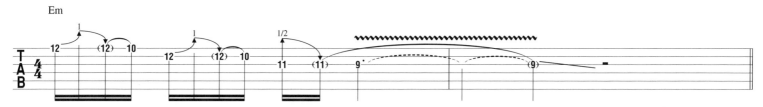

Lick 9, Variation 1

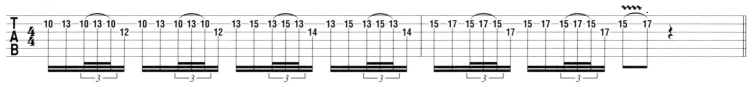

Lick 9, Variation 2

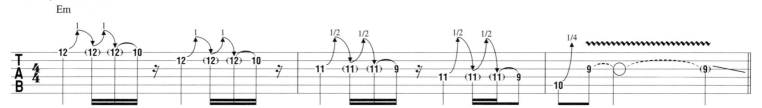

Lick 10

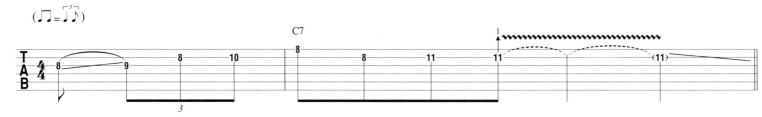

Lick 10, Variation 1

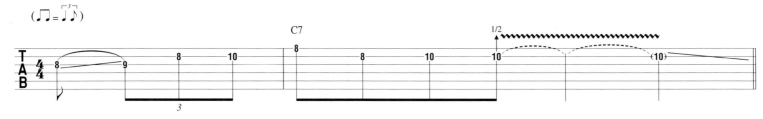

Lick 10, Variation 2

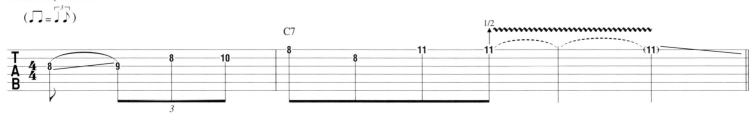

Lick 11

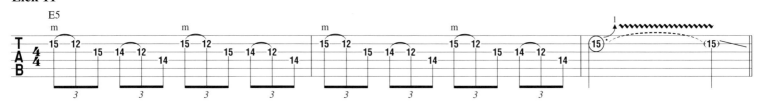

Lick 11, Variation 1

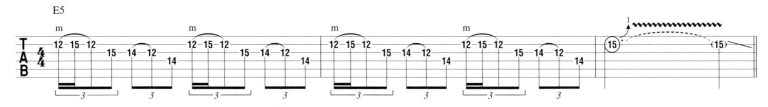

Lick 11, Variation 2

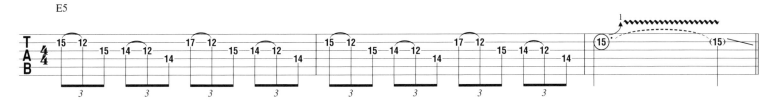

Lick 11, Variation 3

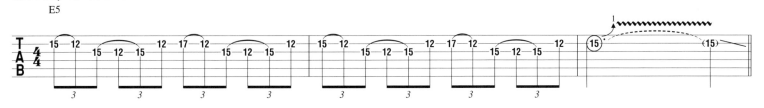

Lick 12

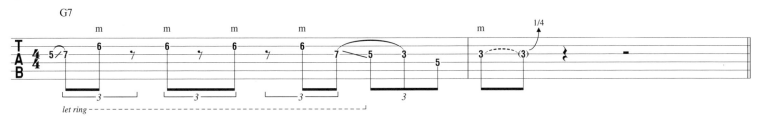

Lick 12, Variation 1

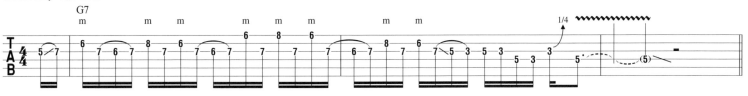

Lick 12, Variation 2

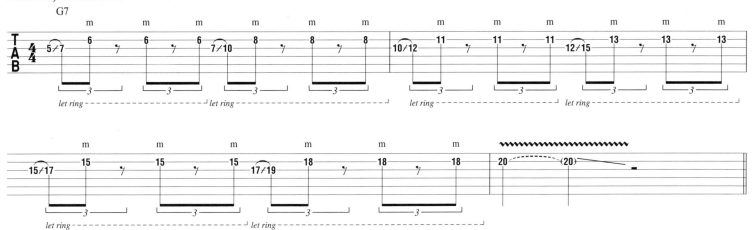

Lick 13

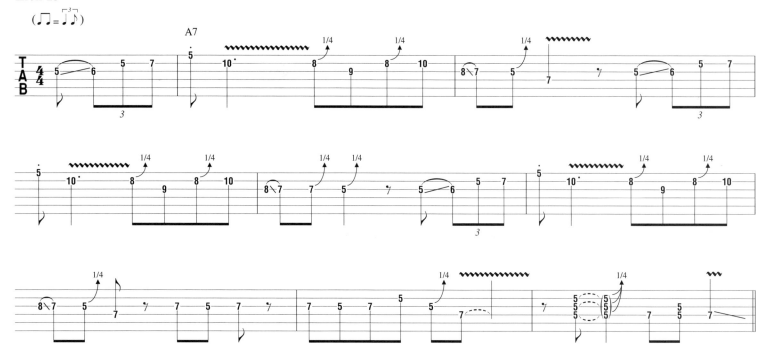

Lick 14

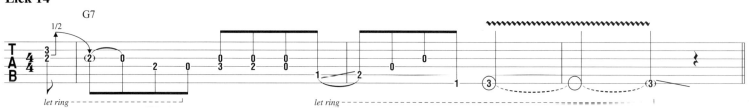

Lick 14, Variation 1

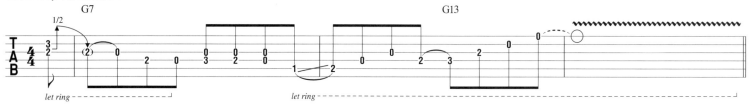